Meditation Guide
For Spiritual Growth

Table of Contents

Introduction

Have you ever felt lost? Disoriented? Or tired? Every once in a while, we experience hardships and are faced with a lot of difficult situations of all different kinds. Significant events, such as the lost of a loved one, career change, starting a family, or entering adolescence, among others, can sometimes make us feel like we're at a crossroad or a dead end. Whether you're feeling lost, unhappy or just want to develop a deeper understanding of the world and everything in it, this book is written for you.

This book will help you practice one of the oldest and most effective ways to reduce stress, develop self-awareness and rejuvenate your mind and body. This is none other than practicing the most fundamental lifestyle improvement — meditation.

When you feel overwhelmed with stress and panic, it is important to learn how to tame and control these through meditation. When you apply and develop the practice of meditation, you will have a deeper consciousness or awareness of your thoughts, emotions, as well as your surroundings. It is important to note that practicing meditation should not just be a onetime thing or phase. It should be applied and practiced in the long-term for you to truly enjoy and reap the benefits it gives to your life. Did you know that some of the most influential religious leaders, CEOs and world-famous personalities practice meditation? They do this to harness their inner strengths, wisdom and overall well being. Famous personalities such as Oprah, Hugh Jackman, and Russel Brand, to name a few, all meditate because it helps them become better versions of themselves.

Oprah believes that meditation helps her feel and become better: *"The one thing I want to continue to do is to center myself every day and make that a practice for myself, because I am one thousand percent better when I do."*

According to Russel Brand: *"I'm quite a neurotic thinker, quite an adrenalized person. But after meditation, I felt this beautiful serenity and selfless connection."*

Hugh Jackman struggled with the symptoms of his Obsessive Compulsive Disorder (OCD) until he discovered the art of meditation: *"Meditation changed my life."*

Keep in mind that no matter who you are, regardless of your situation or struggles, you can practice meditation to quiet your mind and see improvements with all the aspects of your life. If you are a beginner, by the end of reading this book, you will realize that you do not need to be at a Zen center or be in solitude for many months in order for you to meditate. As you read on, you will discover that by undertaking the simple meditation techniques discussed throughout this book, you will be more resilient to stress and gain a deeper understanding of yourself and everything around you. I hope that you'll enjoy reading!

Discretion: I am just a passionate student of health and wellness and am looking for the most cutting edge strategies that can benefit my life, which inspires me to share this knowledge to anyone willing to listen.

Author's Note: I realize that my work will not resonate with every reader. As a man committed to constant and never-ending improvement, if you have any <u>constructive feedback</u> that you would like to offer, or feel like the content in my book can be <u>improved</u> in any way, please leave an honest review at the end of the book.

Chapter 1:
Getting Started with Meditation

"*Meditation is the dissolution of thoughts in eternal awareness or pure consciousness without objectification, knowing without thinking, merging finitude in infinity*" ~ Voltaire

If you haven't tried meditating yet, you are missing out on a lot. This is because meditation is one of the simplest and fastest ways to feel calm and have a clearer mind to make better judgments in your life. Meditation allows you to tap into your inner self and develop a deeper connection in order to reduce stress and feel more relaxed. Before we move onto the process of how you can start meditating, it is important to be familiar with the basics of meditation:

1. Meditation should not be forced

Can you remember an instance where you could not sleep no matter how hard you tried? The same goes for calming or quieting the mind. You cannot actually demand that your mind be tamed but you can create an environment that is conducive to meditation, and thus find calm. When you are able to put yourself in a condition that fosters a quieter mind, meditation will naturally occur.

2. Meditation must be developed as a habit

As a beginner, it is important to remember that developing the habit of meditating is essential for you to be truly aware of your thoughts and whole being. Doing so will help you normalize and release stress in the midst of nerve-racking situations.

3. Meditation is simple but not always easy

Although closing your eyes, sitting in a comfortable position, and deep breathing may appear simple, a lot of people still struggle with practicing meditation exercises daily. Most people who have tried meditating usually fail to incorporate it into their daily routine. For you to successfully develop the habit of daily meditation, you need to find the technique that works best for you and be disciplined enough to deepen your meditation practice.

Different Kinds of Meditation and Relaxation Techniques

A. Guided Visualization

Guided visualization is simply imagining yourself in a serene and relaxing situation. By forming clear or vivid images of your happy place, you can gradually work your way out of rather stressful circumstance and find yourself in a more peaceful place and time. You have many guided meditation resources available to you online and you could either listen to an audio podcast, or get an expert on a YouTube video to help you visualize more effectively and be relieved from stress.

B. Mindfulness Meditation

Mindfulness is basically having a heightened awareness or consciousness of the things that are going on around you. It is also focused on helping you live in the moment and not be affected by your past or your future worries.

C. Transcendental Meditation

Transcendental meditation involves the uttering of a mantra to get rid of distracting thoughts. This natural technique will help you enter a relaxed and calm state of mind and inner peace.

Other forms of meditation include yoga, Tai Chi and mantra meditation. Regardless of how you meditate, as long as it helps you have a more relaxed mind and body, and it works for you, do not stop doing it. By building your meditation skills, you will be able to maintain a certain balance and protect yourself from the stressors of ordinary life.

Tips to Get You Started

1. Constantly remind yourself of your goals and purpose

One of the key ways to starting and maintaining a new practice is by reminding yourself of your purpose and objective. Ask yourself these: Why am I doing this? Who am I doing this for? When you are able to be clear on your goals, you are more likely to continue in pursuing them especially in the long term.

2. Know what works for you

When you are just starting to meditate, do not be afraid to experiment with the technique that will work for you. You can try sitting down with your eyes closed, or standing up with bare feet and keep your eyes wide open. Regardless of how you meditate, as long as it helps you be more aware of yourself and surroundings do it.

3. Be Committed and Consistent

One of the best ways to form the meditation habit is by having a specific time and place to meditate. But keep in mind that you don't always have to be in that same spot for you to be able to meditate. The purpose of having a predetermined time and place to meditate is just to help your mind and body get used to your new routine. As you gradually incorporate this into your life, you will be able to meditate wherever and whenever, in no time at all.

A Simple Meditation Guide

1. Drop whatever you are doing and set your timer for 5-10 minutes

2. Find a quiet spot where you can sit on a comfortable chair with your feet flat on the floor and your back straight.

3. Remember your goals and purpose for meditating.

4. Start being aware of your breathing, take deep breaths slowly and close your eyes

5. Feel your senses from your head to your toes and observe whatever emotion you are feeling.

6. Inhale, exhale, and notice how your breath flows in and out of your body. Count from 1 to ten as your breath rises and falls. Do it slowly and focus on your breathing.

7. When you hear your alarm go off, continue breathing normally and notice your posture, thoughts and feelings after this simple exercise.

8. Slowly open your eyes and let your body go back to its usual rhythm.

Note that this is just a basic guide to help you get started. There are actually a lot of other techniques and exercises that you could try.

Chapter 2:
Benefits of Meditation

The benefits of meditation cannot be stressed enough. These range from having a healthier mind and body to developing stronger and deeper relationships. In this chapter, you would see how meditation could significantly make you feel happier, satisfied and more content with everything that is part of your life.

When you meditate, you should:

✓ **Have an improved focus**

Meditation can give you more concentration or enhanced focus because it allows you to be familiar with your thoughts and thinking patterns. It can significantly help you increase your attention span and level of awareness because it helps you discover your main and real source of energy.

✓ **Be more creative**

Meditation also promotes a person's creativity because meditation enables a person to come up with original or novel ideas. It helps an individual think outside the box and transform his ideas into a reality.

✓ **Be more compassionate and understanding**

By meditating, people are also able to show more understanding and have a generally better mood because meditation helps increase positive emotions and decreases negative ones.

✓ **Reduces stress**

One of the greatest benefits of meditation is that it reduces stress and helps individuals stay calm while under pressure. This is because meditation helps normalize your blood pressure, breathing and heart rate. With enough practice, meditation could also help you have peace of mind. You will also feel empowered because, through meditation, you can have the power to regulate your thoughts and emotions.

✓ Have a healthier lifestyle and stronger immune system

The physical and health benefits of meditation are abundant; it does not only boost your immune system but it also helps you to adapt a healthier lifestyle. Studies have shown that people who are trying to quit smoking or give up excessive alcohol drinking have found it easier to control their habits when they meditate.

✓ Make you feel happier and more content

We all want to be happy. Fortunately, meditation can help us feel more alive with overflowing joy, energy and contentment. For thousands of years, this simple technique has been proven to positively impact a person's mind and body and make him feel happier and healthier. Once you have learned and mastered the skill of meditation, you will experience positive emotions and happiness like never before.

Chapter 3:
Meditation for Spiritual Growth

Spirituality is basically defined as *"being connected to something greater than oneself"* as well as reaching or attaining a higher level of consciousness. One of the most important factors to enable a person to live life to the fullest is to understand that every aspect of his life is balanced and is in perfect harmony with each other once that calmness of meditation is working. People who want to move towards having a more balanced life usually go on a spiritual journey to search for a deeper purpose and meaning in life. Most of them turn to a higher being or develop a deeper connection with nature or the arts. Regardless of how you choose to live your spiritual life, the best medium for developing a greater sense of yourself and the universe is through meditation.

Throughout your life, you may have asked question about your identity, purpose, and life in general—why am I here? How can I live life to the fullest? As you go on your quest in search for your inner being, you are actually growing spiritually. When you are able to experience spiritual growth, you are more likely to see life from a different, more positive perspective. You are also able to break free of your fears and anxious thoughts because your state of mind is no longer easily influenced by your past, present, and future circumstances. You become stronger and more centered. Since being spiritual is essential for us to attain or maintain balance in life, we have to constantly strive for spiritual growth. Here are some strategies on how you can become more spiritual:

1. Have Some Alone Time

The chaotic, hustle and bustle of everyday life can sometimes cause us to forget the importance of taking time for ourselves.

Every now and then, you must spend some time in solitude to refresh and rejuvenate your mind and body. You can take a nice long bath, read a good book, or watch your favorite feel-good film.

2. Be More Grateful

A lot of us are more blessed and fortunate than we think. Because of our obligations at home and work, we tend to overlook a lot of things, especially those things that are right in front of us. The little things or life's simple pleasures often go unnoticed until they fade away and eventually vanish. You can experience spiritual growth by practicing gratitude every day. Think about this for a moment; when was the last time that you were thankful for having a roof above your head, or the fact that you are not lying in a hospital bed? By being more grateful, you will see the world in a more optimistic light.

3. Make Happiness a Habit

When you make happiness a habit, you will not only improve your life, but it will also help shift your mindset and perspective to a more positive one. The great thing about our brain is that recent neurological studies support the idea that we can actually rewire it to increase our level of happiness. We can do this by training the brain to constantly think happy thoughts. You can make happiness a habit by doing simple things such as writing down at least three positive things daily or by always seeking to see the good in every situation.

4. Practice Mindfulness

When you want to become more spiritual through meditation, you must be able to practice mindfulness. Being mindful means having a conscious awareness of your thoughts, feelings, and your environment. When you are able to put mindfulness into practice, you will be able to focus and enjoy each of life's precious moments.

5. Meditate Daily

Meditation is regarded by many as the most fundamental habit because of its ability to radically change an individual's life for the better. A lot of people have gained inner peace, a clearer perspective and significantly reduced their anxiety because of meditating daily. In the previous chapter, you have learned that people who meditate are able to significantly reduce their stress, improve their immune system as well as their overall health. In addition to these benefits, daily meditation can help you become more conscious and experience a spiritual growth that is genuine and progressive.

By making an effort to develop and cultivate your spirituality, you are consequently moving towards having greater joy and happiness in life. No matter who you are, or what your situation is, it is never too late to enhance your spirituality and experience growth through meditation.

Chapter 4:
Meditation for Relaxation

Meditation is one of the most effective ways to reduce stress and anxiety. This is because, through meditation, we are more able to be mindful of our thoughts and emotions. We tend to have more control over our feelings and not be easily overwhelmed by them. Meditation can also be an instant relief from your hectic and stressful life because it literally requires you to take some minutes off to unwind, normalize, and settle your thoughts.

Feeling anxious, worried, or tensed from time to time is acceptable especially if a person knows how to cope with these feelings and manage his anxiety properly but a lot of us struggle with coping with the stress that we experience every day. Keep in mind that stress, at a certain level, is essential for survival. But, when it becomes chronic and overwhelming, it will greatly affect the quality of your life. Fortunately, there are a lot of techniques that can help us effectively cope with anxiety. You can actually use meditation to relax and ease your anxiety. Instead of grabbing that bottle of beer or tub of ice cream for comfort, try these suggestions to help you stay calm and relaxed in stressful situations:

1. Get some fresh air

When you are stuck at a long and stressful meeting or when your nerves are starting to get the best of you when you about to deliver a big speech, pause or stop whatever you are doing and take a few minutes to yourself. It is important to pause for a while when you are feeling overwhelmed for you to be able to calm yourself and control your anxiety. Grab a minute or two to close your eyes and pay attention to your breathing.

2. Practice Breathing Exercises

As you are taking a few minutes off from a stressful situation, observe and be more aware of your senses. Pay attention to your breath by noticing how it flows in and out of your system flawlessly. Take deep, slow breaths and focus your attention on pleasant thoughts. Inhale through your nostrils and exhale through your mouth.

3. Make yourself comfortable

Be in a position where you are most comfortable. You can sit with your back straight as you close your eyes and breathe slowly. As much as possible, do not lie down because you might fall asleep. Loosen your tie, remove your shoes loosen whatever piece of clothing you need to make you feel calmer. Stay in a relaxed state for a few minutes and you will feel instantly refreshed to take on the rest of the day.

4. Close your eyes and focus on an object or scene

As you meditate, concentrate on thinking of a beautiful memory, the scene of your dream destination or fixate on an object in your surroundings. When you are able to have a point of focus, it will help you improve your concentration and mindfulness. When you imagine yourself in a serene and peaceful place, your worries and anxious thoughts will slowly fade away.

5. Enhance your visualization

An instant relief to a rather nerve-racking situation is visualization. As you transport your mind to a peaceful place, make sure to use all your senses to make it as vivid and realistic as possible. For example, you can go back in time and visit your favorite ice cream shop when you were a child. As you go to that happy place, notice the little details, walk slowly, taste your favorite chocolate sundae with sprinkles and remember how relaxed and stress free you were during those years.

As you can see, you can use a lot of strategies to relieve stress. You can relax anytime and at any place as long as you practice the meditation exercises that best work for you. You can relax even if you are not in front of the TV or getting your nails done at the salon. You can combat everyday stress by simply practicing these relaxation techniques.

Chapter 5:
Meditation for Concentration and Visualization

C alled concentrative meditation, this is a technique that is unique because it is meant for you to focus on one single point. The point can be anything that is meaningful to you. It can be an object, a light, a sound, a word, or your own breath. In fact, the object does not necessarily have to be in the outside world, it can be a visualized object inside your mind.

Take note that concentrative meditation is a technique that is usually reserved for advanced meditators. This is because great discipline in needed to be able to be immersed fully in the experience of singular focus. However, with practice, even beginners can experience the serenity of this type of meditation.

To begin, you need to achieve small successes instead of aiming for one great achievement. Train your mind to focus. Choose the object of your focus. In this case, you can begin with a lighted candle. Put yourself in a room free from distractions. Remove any source of noise or stray lights. Make sure that any electronic devices are turned to silent. Schedule this meditation in a relatively free day. Any pending tasks, chores or deadlines are causes of disruption in the mind.

Now is the training. If you are a beginner, give yourself short term goals of achieving focus for 1 whole minute. This may seem short for you but when you are meditating, you will find awareness shifting to somewhere else. Your mind needs to be able to stretch its patience and discipline. Think of your attention as a muscle that cannot be expected to lift heavy weights at the beginning of training. Instead, it must start with lighter weights and progress to heavier and heavier weights. When the muscles have been broken, repaired and trained, that is when it becomes stronger.

The same goes for training in concentrative meditation. You need to work with lighter weights or in this case shorter durations of concentration. Take note of the qualities of true concentrated meditation. All of your focus, mental faculties and awareness are wholly centered in the object of the focus, there are no associations, no interpretations and no other thoughts aside from the object. This is how difficult this type of meditation is but, with training, you will achieve it.

Do not be discouraged when your mind wanders away from the object. Even experienced meditators have these momentary distractions during meditation. The mark of discipline is not only how long you are able to maintain the focus but also on how efficiently you are able to rein back your attention when your mind wanders.

To help you focus, here are some ways to guide your mind during concentration, in this case the lit candle:

Focus on the flame, look at the colors, the outer flame that is orange and then red. Move towards the inner flame, which is bluer and hotter. Look at how the wick is black and firm and standing in the pool of wax. Notice how the flame flickers and creates wisps of smoke as it moves. Feel the warmth of the flame and allow it to fill your mind and body.

Realize how the more focused you are on your concentration, the more serene you feel. There are no noises, no sights, no lights and no distractions. There is only the flame and you. As your eyes are focused on the flame, notice how, in some way, the flame merges with your vision and your vision is merged with your mind and your mind with the rest of your body. You will soon feel very light as if you are one with the flame. When it flickers, you sway. When it creates wisps of smoke, it is you exhaling. As it stands on the wick, it is you sitting on the floor. As it expands, you also expand your horizon. As it narrows, you become more focused on the flame. There is no longer a distinction between you and the flame, your mind and the flame is one. Feel this oneness with the flame filling your entire being. Feel how completely free your mind is despite being constrained in your physical body.

When you notice that your mind is floating away from its focus and it starts to follow random ideas, associations or thoughts, rein your focus back into your control. Do not pull it in abruptly. Instead, do it calmly and gently. Just like a muscle carrying a weight, you lift it slowly, your muscles contract to the point of pain but relax while adjusting to the rest. Do it the same way for refocusing.

Once you are thinking about something else rather than the flame, reel your focus again. What were the thoughts before you strayed? The candle. Where are you now physically? In the floor, with your legs crossed and your palms on your knees. Where are you now mentally? Focusing on the candle. Which part of the candle? The wick. Which part of the wick? The flame. What are you focusing on? The flame and only the flame.

Give yourself an additional 1 minute for every session of concentrative meditation. As you progress, your concentration muscle become stronger and stronger and it becomes more patient and sharper than ever. Soon you will discover that you are able to prolong your concentration to hours until you are no longer aware of the hours or the time at all.

Chapter 6:
Meditation for Mindfulness & Body Scan

A meditative technique associated with mindfulness, this is somewhat the direct opposite of the concentrative type of meditation. While concentrative meditation is all about focusing on one object and reining back your thoughts as they wander to another idea, mindfulness meditation does the reverse. In mindfulness, you not only have no object of focus at all but you also allow your mind to have thoughts that wander.

Before practicing mindful or mindfulness meditation, you need to know what mindfulness is all about. Being mindful or having mindfulness is about your capacity to be aware of the inner world within you and outer world around you. It is being aware of not only physical objects or those that can be seen by your eyes or felt by your senses but also being mindful of your body, the inner workings of your body, your emotions and the situations that trigger or do not trigger them and the thoughts of all life events.

The necessity for mindful living began with the idea that people today are missing out on certain details in their lives, which in turn prevents them from living a full life. This is because the world today puts a premium on the ability to multi-task or to do several things at the same time, which often results to spreading your awareness too thinly over too many things so that you end up not experiencing anything at all.

For example, when having lunch at the office, you may be checking your email, talking to your colleague and preparing for a presentation in the afternoon. You are doing three different things at the same time on top of actually having lunch. As a result, the satiation that you are meant to experience with lunch is not achieved. You end up eating more than you should and the other work that you are doing also suffers in quality.

This is the reason why mindfulness has found its application in not only meditation but also weight control and health, time and task management, professional development and other contemporary applications. In the same example of eating lunch, studies show that people who focus on their eating, pay attention to the taste, texture and the nourishment they receive from the food are more likely to feel full than those who multi-task. People, who dedicate a few minutes in a day to mindfulness feel better.

The intention of mindfulness meditation is to allow you to experience every thought and experience it at its fullest. You allow your awareness to permeate every detail of that thought until you have fully explored it to its minutest detail. Take note that you are discouraged from adding opinions, values or judgment in the thought.

For example, your thoughts drift to your workplace. As you immerse your awareness with the thought of the workplace, do not allow yourself to make judgment calls such as your boss in too demanding, your colleague is worthless or your output is lacking in quality. You are only encouraged to be just aware of the thoughts, nothing more and nothing less. You are only meant to know that the thought is there.

The essence of mindfulness meditation is that it will help you observe how you observe. Imagine yourself thinking on these thoughts but at the same time, you are detaching yourself and watching you as you think. The idea is to see how you think. When you are aware of how you think, beyond what you think, then you are nearer the state of mindful meditation.

When you have these objective and detached observations, you will see the patterns of your thoughts. How do you perceive things? How do you value people? How do you associate a person, thing or event with another thing? How do you determine which is good and which is bad? How do you use your senses? Do you favor certain senses over the other? Do you usually ignore audio cues or scenarios and put too much focus on visual cues? What is the pace of your thinking? Is it too fast so that you overlook certain things or too slow so that you get lost in details and are unable to move forward? Which events trigger which states of your mind? How do you see yourself, loved ones and acquaintances? What makes you happy, sad, angry or indifferent?

Remember, you are not making judgments. This is all about observing your thoughts and allowing yourself to observe you as you think. You can borrow from the skills you have learned in concentrative meditation when you get lost in judging thoughts. When you find yourself making opinions, comparing one thought to another or making and finalizing judgments, you need to stop and rein your awareness back into a neutral state of observation.

Take note, mindfulness meditation is not limited to the usual sitting in a room with legs folded. This kind of meditation can be done almost anywhere and anytime. From eating, to exercising, to working and to other activities, mindful meditation can open your awareness and immerse you into the experience of daily but still important events and ideas in your life.

To try mindful meditation, you can use a beginner's approach, which is the classic sitting alone in a quiet room. This meditation does not require alteration of your breathing as the entire purpose of mindfulness is to give you an awareness of your present self and all current actions. Breathe as you would normally and do not put any value into the breathing, as being good or bad. Next allow your mind to wander. You will most probably encounter thoughts about memories, upcoming events, movies, loved ones or any other random thought. Do not attempt to achieve a blank mind, remember these thoughts are important, even random ones. Your goal is to be aware nothing more.

Chapter 7:
Meditation for Transcendence

Founded by a well respected guru, Maharishi Mahesh Yogi, transcendent meditation or TM is a unique form of meditation. To understand the technique of TM, you must first understand the background of its founder. Born Mahesh Prasad Varma, the circumstances during his early life are still widely debated because traditionally, when a boy enters as a monk, all family relations are dissolved. Mahesh came from an upper caste family and enjoyed the privileges of education and prestige. While different accounts suggest that he was employed in several roles, some say he was a government officer while some say he was an educator, none can dispute his eventually discipleship with Brahmananda Saraswati, another well respected guru of that time.

As soon as he entered his role as a student, he changed his name to reflect his decision to leave the worldly life and begin life as a monk and pursue spirituality. Due to his dedication and loyalty, he was writing on behalf of his teacher and also making public speeches on the teachings of Buddhism. Before the death of his teacher and because he was unable to inherit the role of his teacher due to Mahesh being of lower caste than the teacher, he was tasked with spreading the meditative teachings to the world.

Mahesh not only spread the teachings but also he made it popular both in the Easter and Western world. He went to India and there started an entire movement called the Spiritual Regeneration Movement. He gained a solid following among the people. From his travels in India, he has received the title of Maharishi or great sage. The title soon became a part of his name on his future travels outside India.

Mahesh traveled further around Asia, from Burma, to Thailand, to Singapore and even reaching as far as Hawaii. When he reached the United States, he was met with a loyal following, mostly of average people but some notable members of an unlikely group, actors and actresses of Hollywood. He also reached European and Oceanian countries giving lectures at various great halls and auditoriums. Of his most famous followers were the Beatles, who they considered as their spiritual advisor. Today TM is one of the most studied forms of meditation and has gained application not only among monks in temples but also among students in universities, executives in corporations and officials in the government. The benefits gained from TM were collectively called the Maharishi effect.

TM is primarily mantra based or based on any given sound. It is suggested that TM be practiced daily for at least 20 minutes with your eyes closed. It is meant to provide you with a way to relieve you from stress, anxiety and give you relaxation and growth. Due to the TN being mantra-based meditation, it is often classified as belonging to the concentrative type of meditation. However, the TM movement suggests that concentration is not vital and the objective is to be very attentive to the mantra.

TM begins with de-stressing phase that goes with taking the time to relax and then at the same time pair it with visualization. You can expect your mind to wander during this phase but this is perfectly normal. However, you need to restore your attention to the mantra.

There are no special positions required for TM but you need to close your eyes as you listen or pronounce your chosen mantra. The words that you choose act as your medium towards downgrading your mental functions to a more simple and serene functioning. As you think or pronounce the words, they enter your awareness to a point that they reach your core brain functions.

Take note that the actual mantras are closely guarded secrets and are only passed on from recognized teachers to students. The founder has developed a variety of mantra and there is a strict criterion of how one student is to receive and use a specific mantra. The level of the student usually determines the choice of mantra. Beginners or novices are often given a starter set of mantra that gradually progress from ever increasing effects of relaxation.

Also, the founder cautions on the haphazard use of mantras. The level of the practitioner does not only determine each mantra but also by the background of its user. For example, the mantra Om, which is said to be used by TM but also by other meditative techniques, is supposed to bring a person greater feelings for isolation. This mantra is said to be useful for those who prefer the life of a hermit or those who prefer to be separated from society. A working professional may be inappropriately matched to the mantra Om and would require another mantra for TM.

There are other speculations on the choices of mantra and how they are matched to the person who would use it. Some research says that it is not the level that is the basis, other say it is the gender, while others say that during the initial stages of the student initiation their responses determine the mantra.

This great protection for the mantras is taken from the belief that words when pronounced create vibrations and it is these vibrations that are considered to be important in TM. As a result, TM is closely studied in the field of euphonics and suggests that it is not actually the words of the mantra that makes it effective but the sounds that it produces when spoken.

The reason why it is called transcendent is because as a practitioner gains access to more and more powerful mantras, their minds are exercised towards deeper and deeper levels of consciousness. As their subconscious mind is accessed easier and easier, the practitioner slowly gains the ability to access the subconscious during a conscious state of mind. It is said when the subconscious is at the capacity of the conscious mind, then awareness is expanded.

With awareness expanded, the practitioner is able to reduce all events and experiences into their simplest and subtlest forms all the way to the source of the thought itself. When this is achieved, there is said to be an inner state of complete silence that results to transcendence. A person goes from various levels of consciousness during TM, from waking, to dreaming, to sleeping, to transcendental consciousness and even beyond towards cosmic, God and unity levels of consciousness.

Chapter 8:
Meditation for Cultivation of Specific Emotions

Meditation is not only for expanding your awareness but also for cultivating specific emotions into your being. General knowledge suggests that emotions are a product of events and emotions are out of your control. This misconception is often reflected by the words that are always used with meditation, for example, "caught," "overcome," "fell," and other similar passive verbs. Contrary to popular knowledge, emotions are not only within your control but also they can be cultivated using your will.

Cultivation meditation comes from the idea that emotions are entirely within your control, if you only know how to take control them and cultivate them. The reason why they are thought of as being outside your control is because you may be unaware of the process that brings about emotions. This is the secret why cultivation meditation is possible, when you are able to understand the true nature of meditation, then you can take control of your emotions, instead of letting your emotions take control of you.

Before you attempt to use meditation to cultivate emotions, you must first understand the way emotions are viewed. Emotions are not actually a set of responses that are born out of habit or out of the regular use of a specific response to a specific event. For example, if you always find yourself surrounded by people who react with envy towards the fortunes of another person, then the more you see the envy, the more you feel it and the more you respond to the fortunate person with envy. Whenever you focus on that person, the feeling of envy is felt. Have you ever been in a similar situation?

Imagine the opposite of the above example. People who are grateful and have a positive outlook in life surround you. You see life in an entirely different manner and, for example, you see that fortunate person, you do not feel envy but maybe joy at the situation of other people. As you may see it is the conditions that prompt you to feel a certain way but imagine what would happen if you could create the situation that would prompt the emotion. This is what cultivation meditation is all about.

Cultivation meditation begins with an acceptance that, like you, all people are able to feel emotions that are good or bad but when there is a choice, they will choose to feel good rather than bad. When you have this belief, go on by understanding that all people including you share a common wish to be avoid suffering and fulfill your dreams. When you have this commonality, you can begin to see the world, the people and the emotions you feel from another perspective.

When you know that you are like other people, that you share the same dreams, you can begin to develop an understanding for them. You understand the reason why they do and do not do certain things. This understanding is an abstract concept but when it materializes in your actions, it becomes the emotion of empathy. When you know that other people are suffering the same way that you are, you feel the emotion of compassion. When you know that other people feel joy the same way as you do, then you feel the emotion of happiness.

Allow yourself to meditate on these thoughts when you are attempting to cultivate a specific kind or set of emotions. If you want to be happy, meditate on the thoughts of how other people feel joy when they are able to fulfill their dreams and when they are able to free themselves from their suffering. Use the joy that they feel and use it as your own. Just like them, you can be joyful. Just like them, you can have your dreams fulfilled. Just like them, you can free yourself from suffering. When you have these thoughts then you will manifest these ideas into emotions, which in this case involve being happy.

You can also create emotions through meditation by visualizing events that create your desired emotions. For example, begin with your usual meditation preparations. Now recall an event that has brought you the greatest happiness in your life. Look at yourself on that event. How does your body move? How do you talk? What does your face look like? What thoughts are going on in your mind during that event? Continue to focus on your image during the meditation and see the happiness flow from that image into your current body. As you allow these feelings to move towards you, begin to picture yourself in the same manner in your current state.

Cultivation meditation is a great and powerful tool especially in a world where emotions are usually the triggers of both positive and negative actions among people. So great is the potential of this meditation that it is believed that the Buddha himself has given a very specific teaching about the use of cultivation meditation. Roughly translated into English, it is the teaching that can be found at this link___

For those of you unable to access the link, the link is written in full so that you can type this into your browser.
http://www.wildmind.org/metta/introduction/metta-prayer

Chapter 9:
Meditation for Self-Healing

Locked within the confines of your body is its remarkable ability to heal itself. The body is always in a state of constantly trying to balance itself. If there are health issues, mechanisms are in place to strive to address the issue, correct them and return the body to a normal and ideal state. However, these self-healing mechanisms become weak over time. You will notice this when you compare previous health situations. You may wonder why sometimes it is easy for you to bounce back from an impending health problem and then in some situations, the illness takes hold of your body more vigorously.

The reason behind these changes is that the self healing mechanism is in itself breaking down. It is no longer able to function at maximum capacity to regulate your health and combat any infection, wound, disease or imbalance in the body. Stress is usually blamed as the culprit for weakening the self healing mechanism. When daily stressors constantly bombard your mind, the mechanism almost slows down to a halt. When this happens, your body is left vulnerable to various types of diseases.

Combating stress is therefore one of the best ways to start to reactivate the mechanism and the very first step that you need to take to achieve self healing is to become aware of its potential. The more aware you are of the body's natural ability to heal it, the more consciousness you pour into every cell in the body. When every fiber of your being is mentally controlled into the self healing mode, your immune system, your cell regeneration and every mechanism in charge of protecting your body and also of healing it in case there are illnesses become more active.

Before you undergo the meditation techniques for self healing, it is important to understand how meditation views illnesses and also health. In this perspective, health is not only important physically but also mentally. It is believed that only when the mind is calm and aware can the body's self healing mechanism be used to pinpoint and target healing into specific points in the body. Growth both physically and mentally is only possible when the mind is healthy.

This means that for physical calm or balance to be achieved, there needs to be mental calm first. Only when your mind is steady, stable and aware can it bring the being to total health. Take note that when practitioners use the word health, it is not limited to the traditional concept of health as a body that is free from illnesses. Health in its fullest meaning suggests the absence of illness and the maintenance of balance both in the body and the mind. Just as the physical body is able to affect the mental aspect of the person, the converse is also true. Your state of mind can also affect your state of body.

This is where the secret of self healing can be found. The link between the mind and the body is consciousness. This is how the mind can trigger the body to activate its self healing mechanisms. It is not a matter of having the mechanisms because those are already within you. Instead it is a matter of making your mind realize that is the key to turn the mechanisms and make it once again useful for the body.

Another concept that you need to learn is the idea of the prana that can be translated as the life energy. Different cultures have different names for this energy. Some call it chakra, some call it chi, some say that it manifests into auras and some simply know it as the life force of the person. Prana or whatever you wish to call it is the basis of the health and wellness of the person. Prana is the energy that determines the health of body and the mind.

The more prana you have, the better your body is. You feel more energy, you are more motivated and you are more alert.

You are healthier and more protected from disease. The less prana you have, the weaker you become, the more unmotivated you become and the more inattentive you respond to daily life. Take note that prana is not necessarily confined within your body alone. In Hindu belief, prana represents the sum total of all energy in the universe, both those of living and non-living objects. This means that during your self- healing meditation you not only rely on the energies within you to heal yourself but you can also tap into the reservoir of energy in the universe to heal your body.

Now that you are aware of the power and ability of the body to self heal and of the energies that you can muster, you are ready to begin your self-healing meditation. Begin by assuming your preferred meditative stance. While you can take any position, for self healing, it is best that you do it while lying down on a flat surface. If you have a lumpy bed, you may consider a floor mat to best support your body.

Next you need to focus on the area you want to be healed. This is what makes self healing meditation unique compared to other techniques. While in other meditation, you are either concentrating on one object so you can

achieve awareness or you are allowed to explore your thoughts as they come into your awareness, in self healing meditation there is a difference.

You use your awareness and combine it with an intention of healing. You use your knowledge combined with your awareness to will your body towards healing itself. Unlike a passive meditator, you assume a more active role in this technique. To achieve this, you can use the visualization technique. There are various ways of applying the visualization technique; the general or specific way.

In the specific way, you are already having a health problem that you want to address. For example, you have a pain in your stomach area. Use visualization technique to picture the area of your stomach in your mind. Feel the stomach and its shape, imagine the blood vessels as they ferry in and out nutrients to your stomach. Imagine the area where the pain is and will the blood to infuse it with more energy to repair itself. Feel the pain as it slowly subsides. It will not be entirely gone but you will feel relief.

In the general way, you may not have any issues to address or you may be looking for something that ails you but you cannot pinpoint it. Allow the visualization process to guide you where the health issue is or where you are most vulnerable for developing a disease. Imagine every part of your body, follow it with a body scan. Feel every portion of your body and subtly allow your awareness to point you to the area that needs attention. Feel the life energy coursing through your body. Start with your head, your neck, your shoulders, your chest, your groin, your left and right arms, your left and right legs, and your left and right feet. Give each part at least 10 to 20 seconds of focus, willing your prana to infuse every part.

Remember, meditation for self-healing is not meant to replace any prescription or medical treatment that you are receiving now. Meditation is more of a complementary solution to your healthcare needs. If you plan to use self healing meditation as a substitute or as an alternative to your health requirements, consult   your   doctor.

Chapter 10:
Meditation Using Vipassana

Vipassana - or roughly translated as seeing things as they truly are - is arguably one of the oldest and most ancient of meditation techniques. It is usually referred to as the technique to achieve insight in the true reality and move past the illusions of the current world. Taught by the Buddha himself to his followers, it was passed on from teacher to student until it became the Vipassana movement. Unknown to many, the modern mindfulness movement can be traced back to the Vipassana movement.

Vipassana meditation focuses into awareness of four major human activities; breathing, thoughts or ideas, feelings or emotions and actions. While under this awareness, the meditation is also used to focus on the concepts of how the world is impermanent, how to achieve insight and how some events create pain and suffering.

While there are different applications of both ancient Vipassana and modern mindfulness, there are stages that are similar across all applications. The first step is exploration of the body, here you will focus on how parts of the body begin and end. It is all about realizing various phenomena as being impermanent. Nothing truly lasts forever, events appear and they disappear and stop existing. Even for expert meditators, this realization can be difficult and will require practice and effort before it can be fully achieved.

As you move towards the second stage, you will gradually become used to the focus required of mindfulness. As you become more and more experienced and disciplined, the effort that you once exerted to achieve the exploration will be gone. It will become easier to the point that it will become second nature to you. After this stage, you will soon experience only the focus and the happiness from the meditation. The final stage is that of pure awareness and focus. There are no more distractions, no more effort is needed and no more false assumptions of reality. The only thing that remains is your access to pure knowledge and the true realization of reality. Eventually, this will lead to the freedom of your mind.

Through this type of meditation, you are able to transform yourself. As you pursue your observation of yourself, you are able to find the link between your physical state and your mental state. As you become more disciplined in your focus on the sensations that you feel using your mind, you will be able to filter those that are only essential in your mind. Your consciousness, as it becomes mature, will become more and more disciplined to the point that it can remove any distractions or impurities in your mind and awareness.

There are different methods to achieve the Vipassana way of life and it is one of the most rigorous. While the rewards at the end of the journey are truly great, there are considerable sacrifices that need to be made. Different schools and traditions have different recommendations on how to perform the meditation and how to prepare for it.

For example, one variation recommends a strict code of discipline that has to be observed within a span of 10 days. During these days, there is a period of abstinence. Any form of alcohol, vice, theft, sexual activity and murder are discouraged. This is meant to keep the mind pure and free from distractions to make the person more receptive to the teachings. Next is the stage where students are required to train their minds into developing awareness. This is where breathing techniques are observed. This is a preparatory phase in the succeeding stages of the training.

The third phase involves the true method; Vipassana. With the person free from distractions and with his awareness muscles trained and ready for the next level of exercises, sensations will now observed in all parts of the body. For every sensation that is felt, the person is expected to react neutrally, no opinion and no association, only the sensation itself. The final stage is a gathering of all those who have learned the stages and the sharing with each other of their lessons.

To begin your Vipassana meditation, start with a few breathing exercises while you are resting comfortably in a seated position. Use your breathing to guide you into developing your awareness. Feel the air as it comes in through your nostrils, through to your lungs and into the rest of your body. Feel as it leaves your body through your mouth and your lips. As you feel it move around your body, use this increased sensitivity to guide in the succeeding steps.

Declare positive affirmations on your part, you may say, "May I be happy and free." Any statement that wishes for your happiness, health and growth will do for this exercise. It is important that before you enter the Vipassana meditation you are truly believe that your life can be happy and you can have freedom.

Next, you are to search for your mind where your true happiness can be found and what it is in the first place. Note that during your journey, you may think that happiness can be found in memories of the past. You will realize that this is not so because the past has already gone and true happiness cannot be found in memories. Next, you may
attempt to find happiness in the future, on the fulfillment of your plans or dreams. Again, you will see that true happiness is not in the future, for the future has yet to come.

The one thing that remains now that can be the source of true happiness is the present. Now that you are getting close to finding what you are looking for, the next step is to look deeper. Begin to identify your sources of happiness. Watch out - money, houses, cars, jewelry, relationships and people are not sources of true happiness. They are impermanent, they will come and they will go. You have to search even deeper. The true source of happiness is something that is free from pain, suffering and death.

The search can be aided by the use of tools, meditation being one of them and the positive assertion being another. Another tool is that you propagate this affirmation and express this state of mind to people around you. For example, if you are in search of true happiness, then during your waking moments, try to spread goodwill among the people around you, regardless of who they are in your life. This means that you need to let go of old grudges and other negative thoughts that only burden your relationship.

Once the mind is cleared from these negativities and filled with positive affirmations, your mind is primed towards finding true happiness. You can move further with your breathing exercises and clearing your mind for the search until you arrive at your insight.

Chapter 11:
Meditation in Motion- Tai Chi

U sually associated as a martial art, tai chi can trace its roots with influences from meditation principles. Originally used as a martial art for defense and the improvement of health and of course of mental awareness, this is also a form of meditation. The heavy influence of meditation on this martial art can be traced to its founders, who are said to be Buddhist or Taoist monks. While the subject of its founders and other circumstances of its origins are still widely debated, no one can dispute the mental calm and physical strength that tai chi can provide.

Tai chi has different styles. At least 5 styles are recognized now and associated with the family who founded and modified the original practice to match their needs and preferences. Of course, as tai chi has progressed and expanded its reach to different users, there are now more variations. Aside from its use as sport, tai chi also found its way in various health care settings across the world.

For example, clinics and hospitals have been regularly teaching the principles of tai chi to their patients. Government has opened tai chi centers that are geared towards the elderly members of society. Also, Tai chi is still being used a sport. The many variations of the sport caused its explosion towards acceptance in the Western world.

Aside from physical health, defense and sport, tai chi is also used as form of meditation in motion. The idea behind its use lies in the concept of energy. It is believed that through the use of movement, the energies flow freely and are also attracted towards the body. The movement patterns are repeated until new levels of awareness are achieved on each repetition of the movement.

Another reason why tai chi is also beneficial as a meditation exercise is because of the breathing patterns that are incorporated into the movement. For example, every position or movement requires a corresponding breathing component to augment the relaxing properties of the exercise. When this is done, tai chi becomes a truly meditative experience that focuses on movement to achieve more awareness.

Today tai chi is being practiced all over the world and is no longer confined to the elderly in the park. The practice is being done in schools, hospitals and other similar facilities that encourage health and wellness. It is found to have results such as health improvement, stress alleviation on top of its benefit as a meditative technique.

There are various way of performing Tai chi. One of the most basic one is the standing technique. First, stand on the floor with your feet spread apart at shoulder width. Bend your knees slightly and raise your toes so that they point towards your head. Hold your head up and keel your shoulders down and relax.

Inhale and exhale using deep breaths. Close your eyes and repeat the breathing pattern until your feel calmed and relaxed. The next step involves you focusing on the area towards your feet. Feel how your feet are firmly planted on the ground. Feel the connection that you have established. There is no separation between your feet and the ground, your feet are like the roots of trees that draw energy from the ground.

When you inhale you can picture in your mind drawing energies from the vast reservoir of energy of the earth. Let the energy that you have drawn up infuse your body with positive energies. Use it to cleanse yourself from negativities and motivate you towards actions and progress. As you use the energy, allow it once again to return to the earth. As you exhale, you also purge yourself of negativities.

This first and basic step is called rooting and it is the foundation of other tai chi positions. Almost all positions begin with this routine of standing on the ground, planting both your feet and then drawing energies from the ground. When you have rooted yourself, you can move further to your first tai chi position.

Slowly raise your left heel and keep your toes on the ground. Bend your left knee slightly to accommodate the raised heel. Lower your waist slightly and allow the other knee to bend. Next, raise your left arm and bring your palm to the front of your stomach. Keep your left palm clenched into a fist. For your right arm, raise it so that your right palm is at the level of your eyes. Keep this palm wide open. Hold the position for a few seconds and then reverse the movement to return your body to the standing position.

As you move to achieve this position, make sure that you do it slowly. As you take the position, focus your awareness beginning on the foot all the way to the tip of your scalp. From the toes that are touching the ground, the soles of your feet, your legs and knees and your waist, you can move on to your stomach, your chest, the arms, neck and all the way to the head. Allow yourself to sway, this shows that you are already in a relaxed state because you
are still keeping your balance.

It is worthy to note that despite the slow movement of tai chi, it actually burns calories, this means that aside from its meditative benefits, it can also be used as a way to control your weight and improve your health. Tai chi is also considered a low impact exercise that can be appropriate for elderly practitioners or pregnant women. As long as you do not have any joint issues, fractures and back pain, tai chi is generally safe.

Tai chi has an impressive background of medical research to prove its benefits against minor and major health problems.

Some of these illnesses include arthritis, heart disease, decreased bone density, insomnia and it is used as a therapy for stroke patients.

Chapter 12:
Meditation in Motion- Walking

Walking is possibly one of the most mundane and taken for granted activities. It is an ordinary action that is not even thought of as an activity at all. It is thought to be something automatic and you will realize that when you walk, you do not even think of walking, it comes naturally to you. It may surprise you that this simple activity can offer you great benefits because it can be used as a meditation technique in itself.

Walking meditation is an offshoot of the mindfulness school of meditation. The same principles apply just as with other activity done in the mindful way. In mindful eating, you take your meal as it is. There are no phones to look at, no newspaper to read, no television to watch and no person to talk to during eating. You simply eat the food - nothing more and nothing less. You savor every bite, every texture and every flavor.

This is the same principle you need to apply to achieve this technique successfully. While it is called walking meditation, it can refer to any type of motion or movement. When applied to walking, you watch every step and focus on it in the most mindful way. You feel every step and breath that you take. Because of its nature being just about movement and awareness, this means that walking meditation can be done almost anywhere. Whether you are going to the office, going downtown or to the park, try walking meditation. As you may know, meditation does not always require a quiet room where you are alone and with incense burning or music playing. This is the same way for walking meditation, you can choose a walking route that is quiet or even a busy street.

While you can enjoy the benefits of walking meditation anywhere, if you are a beginner, it is recommended that you first choose a path is as quiet as possible. You need to minimize as many distractions as possible to bring yourself into that mindful state. Again, any place can be used as a route but for the purpose of learning or disciplining yourself to walking meditation, it is best that you start with beginner routes.

Again, you do not need to wear anything special to try walking meditation. However, it is recommended that you wear loose clothing and comfortable shoes so as to keep your mind neutral and avoid discomfort from tight clothes or heavy or high shoes. Remember, aside from the actual walking you also need to watch out for your breathing as part of the meditative exercise.

Begin your first step, take it as slowly as possible. Feel the knees in your legs as they bend and extend. Notice every bone in your leg as it supports the rest of your body into the position that it is taking. As soon as the soles of your feet rest in the ground, feel the weight of your body as it is being supported in place by your feet. Feel the ground with your feet, appreciate every bump and crack that you feel in the sole of your foot, as it feels the ground beneath you.

Take the next step forward. Keep your pace slow. There is no hurry, you are in no rush to reach a destination, to finish an errand or to complete a route, you are simply there taking one step and another, slowly, relaxed and calmly. You are silent, your mind and your body are only aware of the step that you take. There is no wind blowing, there is no light glaring and there is no one that is distracting you. It is only you and the step and the walk.

As you free your mind from every distraction, gradually let go of any anxiety, stress or worry that you are carrying with you. Just as the wind, light and other things are only distractions that you have let go you can do so too with these stressors in your life. Release these from your mind and marvel at the peace that you are slowly feeling while you are taking one step to another.

Move your feet, one towards the other, repeat the pattern. Slowly, surely, silently and peacefully. Feel the pattern that you are using. Use the same way that you observe the way you breathe during meditative breathing exercises but this time with walking. Feel as your body moves, the muscle contract and relax. Feel the movement. Feel the moment.

Visualize each step that you take as something that brings you joy, peace and hope. If you would like to associate this movement you are taking, it is said that the Buddha himself, as he took his first steps either after being born or after achieving Enlightenment, with every step that he left, a lotus flower bloomed on the spot. Use this visual as your guide, every step you take, you remove the pains and suffering of your mind. Every step that you take brings forth only awareness and peace. Soon you will notice that you are no longer taking a path or following the route that you intended to take.

Walking meditation is completely devoid of intention or objective. You are not walking so you can somewhere, you are not walking so you can exercise and as you progress, you are no longer walking so you can meditate. You are walking just for the sake of walking and you are in full awareness of having a mind that is filled with nothing other than peace.

As you move, you will soon develop insights. Each person will have a different insight when they walk. Some realize that their living is all about being in the moment. Just as you are feeling every step that you take, the same goes for life. The moment your other foot leaves the ground, it is your other foot that is now standing on the ground. That is the present. This is the same for life, life is in the moment. There is no life in the past, simply because that time has ended and you are now on the current time. There is no point in dwelling in the past or focusing your awareness on things that have already gone.

In the same way, you do not focus your attention on the past, you will also realize that you cannot focus on the future. You have no way of being aware or mindful of the next step that you will make because it has not yet occurred. When you focus in the present, you are able to shed worries about the future because you know that regardless of how many hours or days you try to anticipate and control the future, only the present is under your control.

Allow every step that you take to become a symbol of letting go of regrets of the past and worries for the future.

Every step is living in the moment and making the most out of it.

Chapter 13:
Meditation Supplies

While these supplies are not essential to practice meditation, most meditators use some of them to create a more conducive environment that is fit for their needs. Each person has a unique environment that makes it easier for them to reach the meditative state or ignore distractions. This section will introduce you to meditation supplies and show you your options in case you need supplies for your meditation.

Clothing, Floor Mats & Venue

At the minimum, you can wear everyday clothes for meditation. You have to choose well what you wear because you want to have as much freedom of movement as possible. This is meant to give your breathing exercises the freedom they require to expand your lungs, raise your shoulders and other non-restrictive movements.

If you prefer to wear clothes that are closely associated with meditation then you have several options. Starting of with a prayer shawl. This is an oversized cloak that you can drape around your entire body to provide you the warmth needed and at the same time the freedom of movement. For men your options are simple white shirts that are loose fitting and with sleeves. They are made of a variety of materials that allow enough air to cool you. For women, you can also have the same shirts but with a more feminine cut. Another popular item is pants that are white and made of stretchable fabric. Kundalini tops and pants are also being worn by women today.

There are also surfaces that you can use to achieve your positions. Some include round cushions and flat mats. While these are important to make you feel comfortable, they are only meant to keep you as relaxed as possible. When you choose from a variety of cushions, try to steer clear for cushions that are too comfortable. Choose only those that offer the needed layer between a hard floor and you. If the cushion is too comfortable then you run the risk of falling asleep.

Benches can also be a better alternative to just cushions; they give you the support you need without necessarily being too comfortable. Plus these benches allow you to achieve certain positions that may be too uncomfortable when done over prolonged durations of time. For example, if your meditation posture requires you to sit on your folded legs, then you need a bench to keep your body weight from pressing into your thighs. A bench will comfortably allow your feet to be folded in a slot below the actual surface where you are seated.

Your venue can also be the place to put your objects of focus. There are different objects that you may use. One of the usual ones is an altar where statues of the Buddha and other revered figures in Buddhism and meditation circles can be placed. Offering bowls that you can fill with rice, flowers and other gifts can also be placed on this altar. Again, take note that the altar is not similar to the altars of other religions. It is only meant to be used a place to focus your awareness and not intended to worship deities as with other altars.

To make your meditation room even more special, you can further include furnishings. The most common are the screens that can be used to provide you with a better space for privacy and a more special area that you can use. There are also prayer flags, banners and other accessories that you can hang around the wall. For windows that are too bright, you can also add curtains with varying oriental designs.

Candles are also important not only as objects of focus but also as a way to make the ambience more relaxing. White light from bulbs is very harsh to the eyes and can only distract you during your meditation. Candles that are often dim yet still provide visible light can make the room more relaxing. Lamps are also alternatives.

Other items that you can add are gongs and bowls. Remember sound is given particular importance in meditation and these items produce unique sound patterns that can create a contemplative mood for listeners. Gongs are usually used as part of a group meditation, often used to signal the start or end of a meditation. It is also used to set the tone or the rhythm that is prescribed by the teacher. For example, every sound of the gong you are supposed to take a breath and the next sound is a sign to exhale.

Meditation bowls are not your usual bowls that are used only for containers. Called singing bowls, these bowls come with a thick metallic rod. This rod is grasped with the hands and then the tip is made to glide around the rim of the bowl. When the rod comes into contact with the edge, a distinctive sound is produced. The sound is very soothing and mellow; it can aid your meditation. Other similar items that are used for the effect of producing sounds are cymbals called tingsha. These are instruments that are usually used for chants, songs and other ceremonies. The sound is believed to purify an area to help the mind focus more on the meditation.

Oils, Incense & Scents
Essential oils are another interesting addition to your meditation room. Each scent is associated with a certain emotion. It is believed that these scents have the ability to trigger a wide range of thoughts, emotions and feelings. Incense also has the calming effect that makes meditation easier than doing it without any of these supplies. While entirely optional, you can purchase these incenses and add another degree of calm over your room. Bowls, where you can stick the incense, can also be used so that the ash will not litter your room.

For example, essential oils that are commonly associated with stress relief and relaxation are vanilla, lavender and rosemary scents. The idea behind the relaxing property of vanilla is that its scent is similar to the scent of breast milk, which fosters a sense of protection and safety. Whenever the mind detects the scent, it triggers the memories of the same calmness.

Lavender is another essential oil that you can consider. You will notice that most products that suggest that they have relaxing properties almost always have a scent or an ingredient that is lavender. It is said to be potent in alleviating sleep problems, such as insomnia, restlessness and other similar health issues.

Finally, rosemary is said to be the best for improving your ability to concentrate. It boosts your focus and your attention and it also relaxes the mind. This is one of the best scents to choose when you are using a meditation technique that requires total concentration.

Remember to observe safety precautions during the use of these oils. Essential oils, in their purest form, are very flammable and irritating to the skin. Make sure that you purchase burners and carrier oils to dilute the potency while still releasing the scent of the oils.

Ambient Music & Audio Guides

Music can also be played during meditation. Instead of songs, hymns or anything with words, the music usually used provides ambient or background music taken from natural occurrences in nature. For example, if you feel at ease with the sound of waves gently cascading in the beach, then you can simply use this type of music during your meditation.

There are different kinds of ambient music available. While some can be purchased, you can also stream videos for free. Your options are wide, from ocean sounds, crickets, dripping water, soft rainfall, chirping birds, waterfall and other sounds of nature. These sounds can be accessed on YouTube or downloaded from major meditation web sources.

Another digital sound that you can use for meditation is audio guides. Instead of you going to temples or facilities that host meditation groups, you can take advantage of audio guides. These are essentially the recordings of a guru, who speaks words that can guide your meditation. For example, if you want to try self healing meditation but it is your first time, you may want to have guide that can direct you towards the proper steps.

Mantras & Sutras

Mantras, roughly translated as holy word or sacred utterances, are a variety of pronunciations of sounds, syllables, words, phrases or a collection of these, called sutras. It is believed that these words possess some kind of power because of their ability to tap into primal psychological force or spiritual power. Mantras are not necessarily grammatically correct or real words at all. Instead, their value lies on the sound they produce and the thought that this symbolizes.

As far as 3000 years ago, mantras were said to have originated in Eastern Asia and can trace their roots to various philosophies including Buddhism and Hinduism. However, even world religions such as Christianity and Judaism possess songs that are already ascribed the same spiritual value as the powers of mantra. In these cases, they are the hymns, songs and other similar tools usually used in music associated with religious ceremonies.

In Buddhist and Hindu schools of thought, mantras are more than words. They become an object of great reverence, a vital tool in any person's quest for awareness. It is also a personal practice, leading to people developing or receiving their own mantras that are unique and can be found nowhere else or be possessed by anybody else. These mantras become symbols of great truths, such as reality, peace, happiness, awareness, knowledge and other virtues.

Some mantras are commonly known and used both by individual, small and large groups of practitioners. Some are shrouded in secrecy, with some believed to be too great to be divulged to the uninitiated. Technically, it does not mean

anything, it is not really a word. Its value lies in the sound that it is produced when pronounced. While there is still a debate on whether mantras are real words. (For example, having real meaning or whether they are truly
 meaningless, being only symbols of abstract thoughts or ideas.)

Some mantras are only sounds or syllables. Some are as short as one syllable. Some mantras are longer than words but fill entire books becoming sutras or scriptures. In between are songs, prayers and chants that are used by studying monks and gurus.

The most common and usually used mantra for beginners is the Aum or Om. Known as the pranava mantra, it is considered to be the origin of all mantras. The legend of OM states that before everything else, before the creation of the worlds, there was a single existence, the One, Brahma. His manifestation, the first expression of his reality was through sound, which was Om. It is this first mantra that is attributed to be the primordial sound and the basis of all succeeding sounds and other manifestations. Mantras can be repeated several times in any given meditation session but there are numbers that bring the best effect. For example, you can repeat a mantra for 5, 10, 28 with the luckiest number of repetitions being 108.

Aside from Om, the mantra for infinity, there are also other mantras that are widely used. Some of them are:

Pavamana mantra

From the unreal, lead me to the real

From the dark, lead me to the light

From death, lead me to immortality

Shanti mantra

Om. Let the studies that we together undertake be radiant

Let there be no animosity among us
Om. Peace. Peace. Peace

Gayatri
Let us meditate on the excellent glory of the divine Light
May he stimulate our understandings

Pratikaraman
I ask pardon of all creatures, may all creatures pardon me
May I have friendship with all beings and enmity with none

The Mantra of Avalokitesvara & Other Bodhisattvas
Om mani padme hum- for compassion
Om vagishvara hum- for wisdom
Om amarani jivantaye svaha- for limitless life
Om namo ganeshaya- for beginnings
Om namo lakshmai- for prosperity
Om namo shivaya- for tranquility
Om namo narayana- for balance
Om tara- for healing

Take note that you are not limited to the use of the mantras listed above. While these ancient and powerful mantras are truly highly recommended for your use as part of your meditation, you are more than welcome to choose from the more modern versions of mantras. Mantra and sutras are words that have special meaning for you. They are often used repeatedly during the meditation as an object of focus. When you use the words you are reminded of the symbolism that they represent.

On the other hand, mantras, being personal tools for your unique journey towards awareness, can also be created on your own. Developing a mantra is in itself a part of your journey. To develop your mantra, you can begin with visualization of your goal in the future. For example, "I will be healthy."

Next, identify the primary reason why you are not achieving this goal. If there are many reasons, then try to think of the one reason that, if removed, could make other reasons go away too. For example, if you are struggling with your health because of making wrong choices in your diet and frequently missing your exercise sessions, then your primary reason could be, "I lack the discipline."

Now, transform the primary negative reason into a positive cause and change the future tense of the goal statement into a current affirmation. The result will be, "I am healthy for I am disciplined." Use this mantra to affirm your success and your journey every time you meditate. If you have a focal point, you can write the words and make it visible in your meditation room. Allow the positive information to motivate you towards success and let the thoughts of your health permeate you during   your   sessions.

Chapter 14:
Daily Meditation Practices

Practicing meditation is not just about taking a few minutes of peace and quiet from time to time. It has to be part of

your daily living. People who have consistently incorporated meditation into their daily routine have significantly

improved their mental, emotional and overall well-being. For you to truly experience the benefits of meditation, you

have to be committed in practicing it regularly so that it will develop into a habit.

The best part about meditation is that anyone could do it. It goes beyond race, sexual orientation or social economic

status; as long as you put your mind and heart into it, no matter who you are or what you do, you can meditate,

develop a deeper sense of self and learn to always live in the present. You can develop the habit of meditating daily

by simply being mindful of how you spend your time and how you go about your daily routine. Most of us

unknowingly go on "auto pilot" mode from the moment we wake-up until the minute we retire to bed. We

sometimes get into the spiral of mindlessly going through our day because our daily tasks have been ingrained into

our system so that we do not need to pay attention to them too much anymore. Our brains are biologically

programmed to encode certain tasks to help us juggle the massive amount of information that we encounter every

day. This is the reason why we do not need to put too much effort in doing mundane tasks such as eating, going through our route to work or school, or finding our way to the bathroom at night. When you practice meditation

daily, it will also eventually become a usual part of your routine.

Establishing a daily meditation routine is simple, but not that easy. You have to have the desire, commitment, and

discipline before you can successfully develop the habit of meditating daily. Here are some tips on how you can start

meditating on a regular basis:

1. Set a specific time and place

The main purpose of having a specific time and a conducive place to meditate is for you to easily incorporate this new activity into your daily routine. You can pick any time to meditate but the most ideal time is the moment you wake up in the morning. This is because it starting early could prepare your mind and body for the things that you have to do for the rest of the day. Also, you are more likely to start the day on a positive note when you meditate first thing in the morning.

2. Be Flexible

Sudden invitations, changes in schedule, and other unexpected events are inevitable. No matter how hard you try to stay committed, there will be days where you have to reschedule or move to another spot to meditate. In these types of situations, it is important to maintain a certain level of flexibility in your schedule so that you will not be discouraged to continue your development when something else comes up.

3. Always remember the benefits

One of the most effective motivators for practicing meditation daily is its benefits. You will find it easier to allot a certain time to pause and meditate when you keep your eyes on the prize. By constantly reminding yourself of the wonders that the practice of meditation could give you, you are more likely to stay focused on strengthening your habit of daily meditation. You can do this by listing down your meditation goals and by posting them in strategic places such as your bathroom mirror or your bedside table.

4. Have a Partner

Having someone to remind you to stay consistent and disciplined in your pursuit of developing the habit of meditation will greatly benefit you. It could also work vice versa. You don't have to meditate at the same time or
 place but, you do have to constantly remind each other in making it a regular practice. When you become accountable to each other, you are more likely to strengthen your commitment to making meditation a part of your routine.

5. Track your progress

If you prefer to do begin or restart your daily practice of meditation, it will help if you keep a journal as you go about the process. By recording or writing down your thoughts, you will be more aware and mindful of the things that are going through your mind as you explore your inner self. Keeping a journal will also allow you to review your experiences months, or even years after you wrote them. This will help you see how far you have grown and matured since you began to meditate daily.

Chapter 15:
Special Topics

Myths & Misconceptions

Due to its increased popularity and its entrance to modern and Western culture, meditation is now being practiced by millions of people across the world. However, some are unable to access the many benefits of meditation because of prevailing myths and misconceptions. Unfortunately these errors only discourage others. This section is all about discussing the widely known myths about meditation and provides you with facts and truth.

Meditation is a religious practice

Closely associated with Eastern religions and esoteric practices, meditation is almost always referred to as a spiritual practice. Most people belonging to different world religions, such as Christianity, Islam and Judaism, may shun the practice of meditation thinking that it is a religious practice that may violate their beliefs.

Meditation is indeed a spiritual practice for those who apply its techniques as a form of expressing their spirituality. However, meditation can be used for more secular reasons, such as accessing its benefits. For example, meditation is known for alleviating anxiety and providing calm and relaxation. This means those who do want to achieve these benefits can simply do the breathing exercises, still feel the serenity but without necessarily associating it with any spiritual practice.

In fact, Buddhism, the most commonly associated religion with meditation is not even a religion at all. Buddhism is an entire lifestyle and a set of practices that does not reflect any requirement of worship or obedience to a divine being. Meditation can be used both as way to express your spirituality and simply just to calm your nerves and get you relaxed throughout the day.

Meditation is hard to do

Another misconception is that meditation is a hard activity that can only be performed by those who study it long term. While there is some truth to this myth because some of the advanced techniques of the practice can only be performed by those who have undergone years of education and experience, meditation is not necessarily a difficult activity to perform. Beginners can just as well achieve the benefits of meditation, without the rigorous training usually done by monks and gurus.

As you may have seen in the previous sections, there are several different types of meditation and more are being developed as the needs present themselves. Some can be done only by experts but some can be done by the average person, who may only be starting to meditate. The reason why meditation is assumed to be difficult is because it is thought that concentration must be achieved.

Concentration or focus is truly needed in meditation but you must not allow the need to pressure you. This is one of the first reasons why attempts toward meditation end in failure, When you try to achieve a goal or reach an objective while you are meditating, you will be too preoccupied by the destination that you fail to become aware of the journey or in this case the meditation practice. Do not focus on achieving something or getting results. Do not be too conscious of sitting in the right position, smelling the right scent or listening to the right background music, enjoy and just be in the process.

Benefits of meditation can only be accessed after several years

Meditation can only be beneficial when you have been doing it for several years. This is another myth that makes people impatient and end up ignoring meditation. The truth is there are both long term benefits, those that can be achieved after years of training and immediate benefits, those that can be achieved after or even during the meditation.

For example, a long term benefit is self awareness and potentially Enlightenment when you dedicate yourself to the practice. Another example is a set of short term benefits. For example, studies show that people who have practiced meditation have gone as far as reducing their anxiety levels and feelings of stress in as little as 2 months of practicing. A more immediate benefit is as soon as you sit, you begin to feel relaxed, more aware and more at peace with yourself.

Because meditation is often portrayed as being done in long periods of time, it is often assumed that meditation requires too many hours from your day. This makes it a very difficult choice especially for people who are pressed for time both at home and at work. The truth is meditation can be done in a span of years nonstop and in a span of as

few as 5 minutes. Meditation can be done when you walk to your office, eat your lunch and even laze around in a park. You can devote several hours to a few minutes to the practice.

Meditation does not heal

Another myth is that meditation is a form or medical quackery that provides no real benefits to the physical body. The truth is some doctors are already prescribing meditation to their patients because of its contribution to addressing stress. One of the main triggers of modern sicknesses today is stress. These stressors have a way of manifesting into the physical world through body aches and complaints. Meditation is one of the best tools to combat stress.

Of course, it is also important to manage your expectations of meditation. It is not a miracle activity that can resolve all of life's worries, anxieties and problems. You cannot replace any current medical solutions that you are taking and substitute it with meditation. It is also not a wonder drug that when done will automatically resolve your health issues.

Also not everybody has the same journey with meditation. For example, some may take a few months to understand and practice its techniques successfully, while others may take years or even decades of practice. It does not mean that one of your fellow meditators have been reaping the benefits of meditation and you have not. Even if you have started at the same time, then it does not mean that you are a failure. Meditation is a personal journey.

Meditation is another form of hypnosis

Another misconception with meditation is that it is equated with hypnosis. Due to the similar characteristics shared among these two activities, it is often assumed that they are one and the same. For example, both meditation and hypnotism rely on achieving a sense of relaxation to achieve its respective objectives. Sometimes, it also makes use of the same positions, such as standing or sitting still. However, it is in these two characteristics that their similarities end.

Hypnosis is all about the focus you need to reach the subconscious, alter it so that changes can be made. For example, if you have phobia of water, a hypnotherapist may bring you to a subconscious state and allow you to work on the fear at that level so that your conscious level will be able to overcome the fear. Hypnosis takes the person back to his past, attempt to address whatever unresolved issues are left from that period so that they no longer affect the present.

Meditation is different. Instead of the subconscious, the practitioner focuses on your inner awareness, your soul and your heart. Instead of the past, meditation focuses only on the present and not even the future. Meditation is all about the now. Instead of trying to change the past, it releases it. It is also believed that the past are only memories and cannot fully control people. Instead of the clinical approach of hypnotism, meditation only affirms and propagates love, peace and joy.

Another point of contrast between meditation and hypnosis is the objective. Hypnosis is purposeful, it is done with an objective. It is meant to be used as therapy, a way to break habits or a method to change negative behavior or enhance positive behavior. It fills the patient's mind with thoughts and sometimes bombards with suggestions. On the other hand, meditation can be the complete opposite. There is no objective and it is not the means to an end, performing meditation is just for the purpose of meditation. Plus, instead of filling the minds with thoughts, the idea of meditation is to remove all thoughts and distractions. The mind is to be poured out of all ideas so that it is primed for insight and increased awareness.

Perhaps the reason why there are so many misconceptions about meditation - aside from the lack of valid information about it - is because of the many variants of meditation. Take note that meditation techniques can be as old as the practice itself but can also be as new as those that were developed in modern times. The important thing to note is that before you let an idea to discourage you from practicing meditation, take time to do you research, validate and then make a decision. Let your experience of meditation decide whether you pursue it or not, do not let erroneous information discourage you from trying it.

Meditation for Children

Meditation is also not only accessible and beneficial for adults but also for children. It may seem unlikely that children would perform, let alone need, meditation. However, studies show that the changing culture and technology of the modern world results to increased levels of anxiety and stress for children.

One of the most prevalent diseases in the world today that are being suffered by children is ADHD. Further proof of early onset of anxiety is that ADHD has been found in children as young as 6 years old. It is this same disease that has prompted Western trained doctors to included meditation in the treatment regimen of children with ADHD. Research shows a marked improvement of those children with ADHD who used meditation. They have better relationships with their parents, family and peers. Their self confidence improves. There are also cases where more than half of the children became more independent from their medication with some completely stopped taking the medication.

When you have made the decision to try out meditation for your children, it is important to convince them to try meditation in the first place. One of the best ways to do this is to show them is that you are meditating yourself. Children are very impressionable and they will try to copy adults or adult figures in their lives. When they see you meditating, they will be curious and will more than interested to try it out themselves. Consider meditating early in the morning and allow them to join you for a few minutes of silence.

Once you have gained their interest, begin to explain to them in simple but understandable terms what meditation is all about. Tell them that you have started using it because of its many benefits and you would like them to have those benefits as well. Encourage but do not force them to try. Most children will jump in on the introduction of something new.

Once you have gained their approval, it is now time to introduce them to beginner techniques in meditation. It is important to start with simple ones that are friendly to their ages. The simplest exercise that you can introduce is simple breathing exercises. By asking them to do nothing else other than sit and just breathe then you are already creating a sense of calm that is important especially for children with ADHD.

Guide them throughout the meditation by doing it with them and giving them instructions every step of the way. For example, ask them to breathe as deep as they can. Then ask them to tighten their lips and exhale as slowly as possible. For children with ADHD, breathing through one nostril and then through another is said to improve the balance between both sides of their brains.

Another kind of meditation that can be made fun with children is yoga. Choose interesting poses with them to keep their attention focused on the activity. One of the most appropriate is the sun salutation pose. Help them achieve the positions by starting with them standing, feet together and palms in a praying position. Take deep breaths while in this pose.

As you inhale, raise your hands to the sky and as you exhale, ask them to reach towards their feet. If they cannot reach, allow them to reach as far as they can without forcing them. Inhale again but now take the equestrian pose. You can do this by bending your left knee and then extending your right leg all the way to your back. Raise your hands. Exhale again while taking the mountain pose, which is hyper extending their buttocks with the feet on the ground and the arms on the ground too creating an inverted V shape.

Next ask them to lie on their chest but support their weight with their palms and legs while tiptoeing. Raise their buttocks and head, they should be facing away from the floor. Inhale and exhale for three breaths on this pose. Now lower their waist until their entire lower body meets the floor but with their chest raised and their palms supporting them in the ground. This is called the cobra pose and done with inhaling. Exhale again using the inverted V shape pose again until you work in reverse, from the equestrian, to hands to feet, to hands to sky until you are back again in your original position.

Another meditative technique that can be used is visualization. This is best done with them right before bedtime and on their beds. To relax them, ask them to close their eyes and guide their thoughts with your words. Paint a picture of something calm, such as a lake that is still with winds rustling through the leaves and grass gently swaying with the wind. You can change the visuals as you deem necessary and appropriate towards the preferences of the child.

Mantras can also be used by children. For children, they will not think of mantras as they are but as songs that they just sing. Nevertheless, you can guide them with the use of mantras by choosing different words that best suit your goal for them of relaxation. Om is one of the best starter mantras that even children can use. Do not control your children by prescribing a way to pronounce the word, let them play around with the mantra. Other techniques can be used for them, such as focusing on an object and other techniques that they want to try that is safe but also beneficial for them.

Of course, children can also be given their own meditation space. This is not only something that gives them fun, having their own nook to try their meditation, but also it gives them an important association. This space will be closely associated to the calm and serenity that meditation can provide. When they are in this space, they will feel the same state because they have become used to the space as a place for calm. You can use this space for example when there is an anxiety episode and then you can bring him to that space to create the soothing effect.

Guided Meditation

Guided meditation is applied when practitioners prefer to be led by a teacher or an expert during their meditation. Take note that beginners as well as expert meditators both use guided meditation. This involves a guide giving you instructions in a soft and soothing voice. It provides you with cues on how to think, what to focus on and which pattern of breathing to take. Guides can also give you mantras and visual cues to help you go through your meditation.

This type of meditation is especially useful for new practitioners who still have limited experience in the practice. For example, if you are a beginner and your mind begins to wander off to another a different set of random thoughts, a guide can help you return to the path of meditation without requiring too much effort on your end. Plus guides have the benefit of experience on their side, which will provide you with many lessons that you can apply later on when decide to perform the meditation yourself.

Below is a sample guided meditation script that you can read on your own to help you during your meditative process. Each has distinct purposes:

Breathing Guide

Let us begin. During this breathing exercise, you are made aware of the power of your breathing. Follow my words in guiding you on how to breathe.

Breathe in for 4 seconds and hold the breath for 3 seconds and breathe out for 5 seconds.

Breathe in 1, 2, 3 and 4

Hold your breathe in 1, 2 and 3

Breathe out in 1, 2, 3, 4 and 5

Repeat this breathing pattern for 4 to 5 times.

Breathe slowly, do not hurry with the pattern. Take your time and experience every breath that you take. If you are having difficulty holding the pattern, adjust to a lower duration and gradually progress to the target number of counts.

As you become familiar with the breathing pattern, being to shift your focus from counting to actually being aware of the path that your breath takes as the air enters and exits your body. Begin with feeling the way the air enters into your body through your nostrils. Feel as it goes into your nasal passages and down to your throat.

As it reaches the throat, feel as it pass to your windpipe and ever deeper into your body. The breath will go down towards various passageways, it starts with large vessels and progress to narrower and narrower ones until it reaches your lungs.

Feel as the lungs expand as they are filled by the air. Feel as your shoulders rise up to accommodate the expanding lungs. Feel as your diaphragm lowers to provide more space. When your lungs are at their maximum expansion, feel the momentary tension of holding the breath.

Now exhale. The air will now leave your lungs and move upwards towards your mouth. It will go through your throat again and then your mouth and finally through your lips. As your purse your lips, feel as the air slowly leaves your lips. Repeat the cycle all over again.

As you have a feel for the pattern, notice how the breaths create a repetitive set of waves that results in a slow and predictable calm. Feel the inhalation, the pause and the exhalation. Feel as it courses throughout the rest of your body. Feel the calm during those brief moments between and inhalation and exhalation.

As you leave the meditative state, do not stand up yet. Instead, feel the relaxation that you have achieved. See how
your breathing pattern has become more regular and more controlled and better than ever. When you have fully enjoyed the immediate effects of the breathing pattern, count to 5. 1, 2, 3, 4 and 5. Now stand up and start the day, calm and relaxed but in full control of your awareness for the rest of the day.

Group Meditation

One of the growing techniques today in the modern world is the application of meditation in a group setting. Take note that this is not a new phenomenon. In fact, group meditation has been in practice for thousands of years and was given by the first teachers who have been taught simultaneously by Buddha himself.

Meditation is indeed about exploring the self and increasing the awareness. However, there are still benefits to be obtained when doing the activity with a group rather than alone. First group meditation allows you to amplify your intentions when you do it with those who share the same objective for their meditation. It is believed that when more than one person gathers together with a similar intention, changes are improved. Second, it also strengthens your connection with other practitioners.

One very important advantage of group meditation is that you can benefit from the sharing of experiences and best practices learned by others. While each of you may have personal paths in their journey in meditation, there are some steps that can be shared. Instead of you having to learn it by yourself, you can take advantage of those who came before you. Plus being in the healthy company of those who share the same interest as you makes you reverberate the positive emotions felt by those in the group. Group meditators feel less alone and feel more motivated when they are taking the journey with other people.

Other benefits include the feeling of physical and face and to face interaction that cannot be achieved with solo meditation. You can share stories about your journey or give testimonies on how you made it work and how others can help you in your meditation challenges. You can feel and create real connections with likeminded individuals.

Another important effect of group meditation is that you are able to create a support group that can steer you back to the path. This is important so that you are motivated to pursue your meditation.

Feedback is also made available if you participate in group meditation. It is common for meditators from various levels of experience to join in on one group with novices. You can benefit from their knowledge and experience. Take advantage of the session by asking some questions that you cannot answer on your own study of the practice.

Finally, although yet to be proven, there is what is called the ripple effect. Studies suggest that when a group of meditators practice, there are waves of vibrations that are emitted and then amplified as these pass from one person to another and to the rest of the group. A large scale study was performed in one area in England. The community performed group meditation and in another area, no meditation was practiced. The crime rate of the non meditators remained the same but the rate of those who meditated decreased.

There are several places that group meditation can be a potential. Aside from a temple, something as accessible as your home can host the group. You can also rent a studio or even a quiet nook in the park can be appropriate for your meditating needs.

Starting a meditation group is easy. It does not have to start big and often the first members of the group will be close family and friends. Find a convenient schedule where everybody is available and nobody is pressured by urgent commitments or chores. Prepare the place for your meditation, sometimes, a floor is more than enough. You can request your guests to bring mats on their own if you do not have enough.

Advise them on the time and place of the group, and make sure that you inform them beforehand of ground rules that you have at your home. For example, they can only change in the bathroom downstairs, the bedrooms are private and they need to inform you if they want to invite other people. These rules make it safe for both you and the other members of the group.

Today, you can only make use of technology to coordinate group meditation exercises. For example, you can use these sites to locate the closest group meditation host in your area or you can announce that you are hosting one. You can also put up a Facebook event or Google to invite to get the ball rolling. Meetup is a popular site that does the coordination for you.

Make sure that you take advantage of the benefits of group meditation by learning from the experience of your colleagues and fellow practitioners. Also, remember that since you are also part of the group, show gratitude to those who taught you by transferring the knowledge passed on by them. By paying it forward, you are able to cultivate more positive energies, compassion and empathy towards others. This is not only what group meditation is about but also meditation in general.

Conclusion

Now that you are familiar with the basic principles of meditation and have learned about the different ways in which you could meditate, I encourage you to apply these steps and go on your journey to having a greater resilience to stress and knowing your true inner self.

Remember that one of the best ways to deepen your practice of meditation is by being involved in it regardless of whether you feel stressed or not. As you expand and deepen your practice of meditation, you will experience how it can help you have a happier and healthier life. As you can see, meditation can significantly enhance not only your physical health, but your emotional and mental health as well. With meditation, you can break free from your addictions or cravings, be more resilient to stress, have a deeper sleep, and a better mood. If you want live with a new and better perspective, now would be a great time to find a quiet spot, make yourself comfortable, and start forming the habit of meditation.

CPSIA information can be obtained
at www.ICGtesting.com
Printed in the USA
BVHW040248030321
601495BV00012B/1399